SLANG*ETRY

The GUTTA * SLANG verses

EXPLICIT

Po·et·ry [pó.uh.tree]-1. Literary works ; verse writing of high quality, great beauty, emotional sincerity or intensity, or profound insight

Slang [slang] -1. Very casual speech or writing: words, expressions, and usages that are usually considered unsuitable for formal contexts

Slang*etry [slang uh tree]– 1. A combination of slang and poetry, with the verbs twisted the way only T.T. King can... **2.** A thought inducing serum of inked verses to stimulate emotions i.e. extreme laughter, intense tears, wistfulness, joy ...

SLANG*ETRY

SLANG*etry -Is the definition of life
broke down to its simplest
with some tears mixed in the ink for emphasis
Mama and dad, told me not to cuss so much
But, I just get so fucking ... emotional
& sometimes things just need to be said
the way they need to be said
And if I can't find a microphone that reach around the globe
- then this shit is just gone have to be read
By all the chicks like me, who people agree, won't ever get ahead
'Cause we have soft behinds and hard heads
and all we wanna do is dream
Slang*etry is for all my way too skinny girls
and the ones who think you're way too fat- if you like eating yo' Doritos girl
there's a man out there - who lives just to buy you a snack
To the hood girls, who commit crimes
'Cause your flower bloomed from dat hood grime
You grew thorns around your petals to protect what was sweet inside
and to keep from losing your mind
because, ambulance sirens were your lullabies...
the devil rocked you to sleep some nights and you were slapped whenever you cried
you might turn into and this goes out to :
All my grown women out there doing jail time
And to the good girls reading this to occupy yo' mind
'Cause you can't get a date
... your morals always get in the way
And to you party chicks that date way too many
Get drunk all the time and get way too friendly
Slang*etry is especially for all my broke chicks, who just reading this
'cause you ain't got no phone minutes
and for my spoiled girls - who got everything plenty
To y'all business chicks that cut checks & verbally slit necks
To my sistahs in the streets who don't know where your next home's at
God has got an angel out there for you girl, believe that
To the deceitful girls that get all you can scheme
You're just missing that one thing ... maybe it's just the right man's touch

♠ ♥ ♦ ♣

And to all y'all who crave the touch of a woman
- some would consider, way too much
To all the new hoes - and the old pros
To all y'all sexy flirty over thirties - and the young swinging singles
To all my widows
To those alternately crying and staring out window's
Slang*etry is for every female who ever read it
and every man who get a chance to see it...
'Cause Slang*etry about us - Every Woman In The World
Because, we mass produce this universe
while slowly stroking this man's world
into thinking it's running us
Slang*etry is so they can see that
hell yeah, sometimes this woman thang hurts
but they can read between these slang lines
and see how we ain't designed to give up..
Slang*etry is a national woman's anthem - slash/survival manual
keep it around for when you need it
I expect every woman in the world to buy my book and read it
.... then pass it around and repeat it
'Cause I wrote this for *all* my chicks ...but, just as much for me
when life got so tight that I couldn't breathe and I had to write myself free
- when people said I couldn't do it my way
and I said, "Yeah, Motherfucker, we'll see"
'Cause I was building us a woman's lounge in my mind
so, all y'all could come here with me...
bring whatever you smoke and yo' favorite drink ...
'cause this shit is like woman's therapy ....
Slang*etry

Nikki You Was So Beautiful

Nikki you was so beautiful- you had big lips and they was yo' real lips
You had long black hair down to yo' hips
And it was your real hair
and, Nikki, you stayed up on the real truth
Until, you ran up on a lie
With that "fresh out of jail" smell
Always talking 'bout his convictions
And all the shit he'd been through
the prison visions he woke up screaming too
said all he needed in his life ... was you
to complete his change
and 'keep him straight'
To us - that nigga was see through
But, you accepted every color he showed you
You took every blow he throwed you
'cause he was like a preacher to you
accept he taught you things you couldn't learn in Sunday school
and made you the main link in his chain of fools
There were obvious signs of abuse
Because, there's only so much Maybelline can do
But under every bruise
You was still cool
And you had a smile every time I saw you
Plenty of laughs every time you rolled through
and you were beautiful ...
Nikki you was so beautiful
To him - his hands around your throat was a method of control
To you - it became a love hold
To me - a wolf devouring a dove
was the only way to describe y'alls love
The deeper he sunk his teeth in
The more you asked me to stay out of it
... So, I did
 I watched you laugh through busted lips
and wanted that nigga's throat slit
But, I had cried my last tear for you ...
I just prayed every day that a change would come through

Plus, he kept you on your knees
so, you was closer to God than me
But, it was plain to see - that you was so beautiful, Nikki
Even when his TKO's
Put you in ICU
He had pushed away your family so, I cried over you
Under all the black and blue and the feeding tubes
You was still beautiful
And ... invincible, indispensable
Because, when I looked at you in that bed
You wasn't you - you was us
You was age thirteen in a park swing
Feet dangling in the dirt as we discussed things
Like the boys we wanted to kiss...
And who was whose boyfriend Michael Jackson or Prince
With our New Edition t-shirts painted on
Remember?
- I had the blue - and you had the pink one ?
I remember how we used to laugh until we cried
And how we cried, when all we could do was cry
'Til we was purified
Like when my brother died
And you damn near moved in with us - 'cause you refused to leave my side
You kept saying that he was an angel now, so everything was gone be alright
The darkest hour of my short life girl, and you were the light
So bright ...and beautiful Nikki
- you was so beautiful
... and when you finally did get out of that hospital bed
He sent you right back in an ambulance
For telling him that you knew
That he got the HIV he gave you, from another dude...
yet Nikki, you was so beautiful
'that with some of the last words off of your lips
You told me to forgive
And with your last breath ... you reminded me to live
'Cause silly me, I never believed that you could ever die...
'Cause I was always the wild one - and you always did right
I never thought I'd pick up the phone and you wouldn't be there for me to call....
Or that your beauty would be so painful I'd take your picture off my walls
And box up your beautiful smile .....crying all the while
"Nikki, you was so beautiful ...."

'Cause the world lost space after losing you
The reason it all happened, only God could have knew
Since, you were a flower child
We buried you in the moonlight
I swear all the roses bowed down when your casket passed by
... The sky opened up and the angels cried
The Weeping Willows shed real tears and the earth sighed
the world stopped spinning cause your beauty had died
or maybe It just seemed that way to me...
'Cause my eyes were guided by misery
So, if you're listening to this poem and you could be Nikki
Imagine your best friend is me
Writing poetry you'll never get to read
Trying to make some peace with your tragedy
Because, if you're anything like Nikki - then we all agree
.....That you're beautiful
And Nikki -whatever star you are when I look in the sky
With my heart calling out and my eyes searching high
You're beautiful
Nikki...you're still so beautiful......

DEDICATED TO :

Those who have lost their lives for what they thought was love
– no matter what the name, place ,date or race
And to you - if you're in a domestic situation, please remember all of the loved ones that you will leave behind for the
hate – wrapped love of one person.
There's always an angel out there, sometimes they come to you
... sometimes you have to go look for them –Seek Help
We all know the slogan, "Love shouldn't hurt."
that's true... *

CHAMELEON

A CHAMELEON is a no good man
.... with a little finesse
He knows how to make you feel sexy - when you *know* you look a mess
Tells you he love's what you've got on - no matter how you dressed
...he's a chameleon
He blends right into yo' skin
From the outside in
So carefully his colors be changing...
The Chameleon
Uses his lips like a paintbrush until the hues set in
Until y'all are one shade completely blended
He builds you sandcastles in the sky
Built from whatever dreams & sweet things you like
He's gone give you everything you want somehow
...he just can't get it for you right now
'Cause the only green in his pocket is weed
The good kind, with no seeds
That's why he ain't got no money to take you out to eat
Don't matter – 'cause he's already blended in
Y'all melded into one person when he first touched your skin
..and he keep's you so fed emotionally
You don't care if you ever eat again, personally
Because, y'all like all the same songs
and he introduced you to some new ones
And he done replaced all of yo' best friends
'cause they ain't go no arms to wrap you in
and keep complaining 'bout what kind of shape y'all in
while the chameleon
understands you and keeps you laughing
tells you to stay home with him...instead
... and lay around in bed
And the chameleon is skilled at blending onto your couch
When you talk shit he just blends his tongue in your mouth
Until you forgot what you were mad about...
Resume his video game after he done worked your body out
And steadily his colors change every day
in different shades

The best colors fade away from his array
'til only his darkest colors are on display
for you...
& you realize you his color changes are becoming mutual
- when he's blue - you are too
- though yo' shade is more true
He's always down and out so - Yo' ass is always tryna help him
& He's his own worst enemy so you always tryna protect him
When he's yellow y'all ecstatic together
Make magic together
& Yo' smile is bouncing off his skin
Yo' yellow is because he telling you, you beautiful again
His yellow - is 'cause the compliments got you to do something for him
& you always gotta have him
So you gotta move him in
'Cause when he's gone you can't stand
...the blackness of his absence
Now you green cause chicks calling his cell phone
Then red again – 'cause your anger gets him turned on
Then black & blue, cause it's you he puts his hands on
Then clear when he's gone...'cause that's the only color that tears come..
So, you pray until the sky turns yellow and the sun turns blue that he'll come back home
Cause' when the Chameleon leaves-
all your colors are gone...

PLEASE DON'T LEAVE ME
(A Ghetto Love Ballad) PART 1

Please don't leave me
Baby...please don't go
If you walk out that door
Im'mo make sure everybody knows that
you take them blue pills
that Benz is rented wheels
And you just a boy still
'Cause your grandma pays yo' cell bill
I know you're angry now - And baby I accept that
This one is all my fault - I'm sorry - I admit that
But, we both understand completely
that your name across my heart means that...you belong to me
and we've been invested since our first kiss - 'cause we were meant to be
We decided on 'forever' way back then ... so we can't let it end like this
& this ain't the first time our thin line between love & hate has been argued
down to non-existent
We fight with every word - heart blows that we know will inflict the most hurt ...
and when that don't work
we use our fists
    usually with me throwing the first lick
        and us breaking up all our shit
            me busting the windows out of yo' whips
              and snatching tracks out the scalp of any bitch you dare cheat on me with
    one second we're locked in death grips in front of the kids
the next we're on our mattress in our favorite ghetto kiss
and after it's all over with ... we realize again that it don't make sense
... but, that's just how our love is - and how it's always been
in the end we're still best friends
- and how many times have we done this
for you to be saying that this time - this is really it?
'Cause, through everything- I never would have believed I would ever see this day....
where I would rather go blind - in that old Etta James moan and writhe type way
than to be standing here watching you trying to walk away.....
though, we've both gotta change if you stay
we can't keep having a different version of the same fight every day
& you can't keep trying to throw us away...over simple thing's
Especially, after all the times I done stood by you

I've been your alibi – more than a few times
lied to the Feds for you
 and went to jail for you
Every time you was the one locked up - *I was the one* who made your sales for you
 - hustled up ya' bail for you
Screwed the landlord plenty of times, to keep a roof over our bed for you
I have personally locked & twisted every single dred on yo' head - for you
I ain't ever asked for no ring to signify me
just allowed you to pronounce and announce me as 'Wifey'
and have literally been here in sickness and in health for you
'cause every single time you've ever been sick
 - I'm the one picked up and fixed your meds for you
The *first time* I cocked a gun while we was on the run – I vowed 'til death' to you
and after all these things I've done - *I'm* sitting here having to beg for *you*
You need some time alone? I respect that
but, when you telling me you *leaving* - I reject that
And I know you're about to ask - that if you're so bad, then why am I trying to keep you?
It's just the simple fact – that no matter what you lack - I still need you
And you need me- to stay this thing on your arm - that makes other niggas wanna be you
-that chick that loves you for exactly what you are – and nourishes your potential
 'Cause wherever you are - is where I still feel most protected
You can't just leave me out here....lonely & neglected
So, boy, go put them bags back
....relax and unpack
Oh - u being hardheaded?
- well, hell- I take my words back
Nigga - Don't let the door hit 'cha
Where the good Lord split 'cha
- You need call Tyrone to pick you up off my porch
 and, here boy - take your kids wit 'cha
Now, don't get me wrong
I know I'm gonna miss you
But for now - don't worry 'bout forgetting my face - I'm texting
you a deuce picture
And a message 'bout how
- I'm through wit cha
You so stuck on being dumb
- that ain't nothing else
- I can do wit cha'
'Cause I'm on some grown woman
two thousand and twelve shit

& if you can't deal with it
You're free to go get some lame bitch
I'm all about my bizness
Somehow, you just don't get it
And thinking about us gets me pissed
So, yeah, boy let's just forget it
That's all you dismissed
You gone be the one who regret's this
Now get ya' fingers out my door -
Before you get your hand squished

PART 2 (A GHETTO LOVE BALLAD)

I watch all the drama right here where I always sit
or looking - like this through my blind slits
'Gotta watch everything out here, 'cause it's show 'nuff watching me
It'll be the same thing next Friday & Saturday
- If it ain't these two fighting again - it'll be Lisa and Randy in 3G
when Lisa find out that Randy got another baby on the way - in building E
'Cause ain't nothing new under the sun...
if you done heard one ghetto ballad - you've heard all of 'em
Love ballads 'round here - are wrote in dark chords - about court dates for child support - and paternity...mattresses' sing out this new ghetto sex R&B....so the chorus repeats..
- The lyrics are about cheating, lies, gambling, addictions, lost hope, ghetto dreams
drama queens, drug fiends, deadbeats
little ghetto superstars whose light may never reach maturity
love tragedies, emotional catastrophe's...& the constant vibratos of arguing
echoing through the walls & the concrete...
everybody singing they part - to the same tune...with the notes gone wrong
on life's broke down piano, with most of the keys long gone ...
and you can always hear it...
Waking and sleeping to it ....until the tune gets engrained in your spirit
The rich folks that ain't dope fiends - can't stand to hear it - 'cause they fear it
They lock the sound behind bars - so they don't have to be near it
...or try to kill it
'cause it's old Cocktail walking the same streets every day
... her hips chiming they wares, advertising her pain for sale
crescendo of the baby's screaming, the ones who need they comfort and the ones who will never receive it - so eventually learn not to need it
little girls lullabying in they childish, grown woman soprano's – for the boys and the men to come & get it if they want it....

lulling they big heads right to sleep and waking up the little heads that don't think...
somebody'll be pregnant by the end of the week.
- Tambourine of bicycle pedal squeaks
 - only the crack head's riding- the kids have to stay inside 'cause it's too dangerous in these streets
... they new toys is cell phones & t.v.
they ringing and videos add to the melody of
 basketball dribbling, sweat dripping like water
 - dope boy's hollin' that they got it
I take my drank outside, after I get my cigarette lighted
'Cause I heard handcuff jangles blendin' in like a violins
 'dem blue boyz out here picking up Pee Wee again -
Bass baritone for me to call his mama and 'them...
     - I probably won't do it though –
I hope they keep him locked up this time - 'cause lately he been running round here acting like an
asshole
 I let his acapella get drowned out by the sirens
 and the fighting
 and the crying
 and the violence
 and the blood that sing out from the grass, when you walk over where somebody died
though most of them lived in vain and died at a young age
... they don't wanna be forgotten
- drum taps of all the footsteps that keep on walking.
Domino clackers, choruses of laughter,
Singing ooh, altogether 'cause Brenda just brought home the new triplets, after having 3
miscarriages in 2 years - and we harmonizing in ghetto ballad unity about - "Oh how sweet God is,
'cause whatever He takes - if you keep faith - He replenishes. With Brenda singing
the loudest Amen
 on top of the tap tap of Sister Black's heels on her way to evening service with them grandkids,
praying all the way, for they mama - 'cause ain't no telling where that girl is
 on top of the alto wail of Chanel downstairs 'cause she done got fired again
 on top of gossip
 on top of liquor swills, & huffs of whatever type of smoke
 until it all swirls together into one note
that you're lucky if you ever heard
and blessed if you haven't
 if you ain't got issues with my ghetto you welcome to come by and share it...
ain't no solo's here but if you want a part on the stage you can have it
& our attention, if you can grab it –
While we create our own singing roles and do our own vocals
in our *GHETTO LOVE BALLAD* ...

I SCREAMED

I screamed into the night
Because no one heard my whispers
I screamed because I had lost my voice
The voice that said – I am somebody
I screamed because the world had told me
That my words didn't matter
I screamed 'til my lungs hurt
I screamed because my heart hurt
I screamed because it wasn't fair
That no one cared that I screamed
I screamed that night because
There was nothing else that I could say….
I screamed for all the things
- that I didn't have and I never would
I screamed for all the times I was hurt
…and had remained silent
I screamed so loud that I scared myself
I screamed because I was scared
I screamed so loud that it shook my soul
I let that scream take control
I screamed so long and hard from the pain
That it sounded like thunder trapped in rain
That night I screamed

Today I Smiled

I smiled because I realized that my circumstances do not outweigh my possibilities
I smiled because I understand that God is the only power in my life
I smiled because I know that whenever a door is closed in my life
Heaven is open for eternity
I smiled because I have my health
I smiled because although my children are the greatest test of my strength they also give me the strength to go on
I smiled because my daughters smile
.... is so beautiful
I smiled because when I look into her face
- which is her father's face
I see her absolute beauty and not his mistakes
I smiled because my son has inherited all of my best attributes
- and made them better
I smiled because I know that I can turn my obstacles into opportunities
I smiled because I have the knowledge to pray
I smiled because I only have five dollars in my pocket
- because yesterday there were none
I smiled because even when I have no place to go
I have the ability to...

NIGGA

Baby, I don't call you Nigga lightly - I call you Nigga 'cause it might be
That thing - that can flip that mental switch
- and make you regress into your black consciousness
Take some of the air out of your arrogance
And make you re-visit a day you never even lived in
when black wasn't just the color of yo' skin
Nigga, it was the part of the bus you sat in.....
It was 'Colored Only'- drinking fountains
It was yo' forefathers who couldn't read or write
But, marched all night, hefting signs that read - 'I AM A MAN!'
And real men like Medgar Evers, who died so you would
Never - ever have to be called, 'Nigga' again...
And since niggas was such a beautiful thang back then
The trickle down effect is that - if we was friends
I would call you 'My Nigga' - as a term of endearment
But, for you I mean Nigga in its ugliest sense
'Cause when you talk to me Nigga - you don't make no sense
You got kids you made, Nigga - and ain't spoke on since
You chase me - like a dog that's done caught my scent
And even though I'm yo' reflection –you -call – me - a - bitch
so what does that make you - Nigga ?
And plus, Nigga you spit lines like a bad rap lyric on repeat
That's why I can't be bothered to speak
'Cause I'm looking past you for a real Nigga
…. A swagger - even when he standing still Nigga
An educate my mind - and keep it real Nigga
A touch me deep - inside my soul....so I can feel Nigga
That can look me in my eyes – and not just at my behind as I pass by
- unlike you Nigga
And I would give you some clues on some things you could do to work on you
But you too impressed with your fake ass jewels
- and yo' whack ass crew's
- and bragging about how yo' baby's mama's - just love to stalk you

- and not getting dirt on yo' tennis shoes

Which − was − made − to − walk − in − dirt

- didn't nobody tell you, Nigga ?

And I feel bad that you so dumb

- but it's got you by this long

I just wish I could reach around all the hoods

- and take all yo' little boys into my arms

- so they don't grow up to be like y'all nigga's

But, I still need to see your beauty in the world's big picture

Now, I might cuss you out - if that's what I have to do

And I might hate a lot of your ways but, I will FOREVER

FOREVER love you

...NIGGA.

CUPID

I try to blend into thin air
So, Cupid won't notice I'm here
I'm tired of ducking & dodging him
'Cause he's my worst enemy
I find him hostile and unfriendly
'Cause he's always shooting at me
Keeps my heart caught and shell shocked
& paranoid 'cause he won't stop
He's the reason I can't even write no love poems
& I don't sing no fucking love songs
'Cause When I find Mr. Right, Cupid turns him wrong
- He play mind games with millions all day long
and he still won't leave me alone
'cause Cupid is stupid like that
He'll put the man I want in my path
- then before I can get him in my grasp
He'll put him right next to a prettier girl - then shoot him in the
ass – and laugh
Then bring me something wack and burnt black
And shoot me in the back - 'cause cupid is an ass
And then sometimes, he'll bring me some sexy thing
A man that fit's me to a T
– meaning - he love the fact that I'm complicated and will do anything to be with me
Have me daydreaming 'bout wedding rings
And then - he'll up and leave me
'Cause I'm the only one Cupid shot obviously
From Anthony and Cleopatra
To Adam and Eve
To - the last nigga I dated - and me
He's been doing this shit throughout history
So, he's better trained at love combat than me
So, when his arrows kill my heart finally
His evil ass resuscitates me
Then he sends his friend Lonely to asphyxiate me
'Til I feel like if somebody don't touch my skin properly
I will literally cease to breathe
I wish Cupid would just let me be...
But, for some reason he always wanna fuck wit' me...

You Make Me Miserable

Cupid shot his arrow in me
he must be blind, unkind or just can't see
That you make me miserable
You shouldn't be nobody's first love
'Cause you make me miserable
and pitiful...
You're selfish, deceitful, and wrong
...but parts of you are beautiful
And the bad thing is that you know
....that you make me miserable
You make me miserable 'cause yo' lips are so ...sweet sometimes, they all I can eat..
And 'cause the minute you get next to me - I'm dreading the second you leave...
'Cause I was broke down on the side of my life's road
starving for love when you found me
and coaxed me... until you finally got your arms around me
My heart got full off the lies you fed me because I was so hungry
phase one in your diabolical plan to forever.... own me
and oh ,your misrepresentations tasted so sweet as they were going down
in your slow ... deliberate doses
because, I was just as cautious - as I was lonely
So, we can both agree, that you tricked me
into melting into this puddle at your feet
& now that your puddle, is my position currently
- you always trying to emotionally drown me
You keep the water deep with these tears you continually make me weep
Thick and murky with your aforementioned, lies and deceit
You make me so miserable some days
That I wish you was a stomach ache
So, I could just throw up all our memories
...and flush this love away
along with the sweet things - the man you used to be....used to say
that keeps me stuck with the motherfucker you've become every day

....demanding the woman in me to love him
in all my old ways
and the fickle bitch - remembers your old kiss
... and obeys
'Cause that phony still uses your voice...when he says my name
Sometimes, the sound is the only necessary foreplay...
Cause, it's some animal, guttural, beautiful, haunting, wanting sound that my soul
always re-plays...
Like a song whose words you forgot, that only I still sing...
When you're making me miserable, I hum the refrain...
'Cause all I still wanna do – is dance through life with you
holding me the way you used to....
I say we make some type of exquisite manure
out of all the bullshit we go through
- which is considerable
I probably won't ever stop loving you though
...even though

𝓤 𝓜AKE 𝓜E 𝓜ISERABLE

UGLY POETRY

I write ugly poetry – 'Cause mostly it's about you
Ugly poetry –'Cause it's true
Ugly poetry –'Cause besides my face, ain't nothing about me cute
Ugly words – 'Cause ain't nothing else I can do
'Cause life gives me an ugly attitude
I steal away & write poetry in the backpacks of runaways
To document they last days
I sit in the black bile
-In the hearts of pedophiles
And write ugly poetry - in ugly tears
Whenever they touch a child
I write ugly poetry on metal
slung out barrels by the devil
Ugly poetry across my t.v. screen
When I look at BET
'Cause them video hoes don't reflect me
Them studio molds don't impress me
So - I write ugly poems about the industry
'Cause the mediocrity distresses me
Then I take my pen and write in dark ink
On dirty sheets - where HIV leaked
For those positively tested...Infected
....for everyone who's been raped or molested
For little girls that leave their wombs unprotected
For every child in the world that's neglected
'Cause all I write about is what I see ....
and when I look around me
It's all... **UGLY POETRY**

I'M A WHINO
- SO WHAT ?

I consume mass quantities of liquor to clear my mind yo...
Straight out the bottle like a whino
If you don't like it don't mind me 'cause I'm fine though -
and quit talking that shit about rehab 'cause I said NO!
'Cause see - I drink with specific intent
To circumvent all the madness and the bullshit
To combat all the sadness and the stress fits
I chug until I'm null & void to the fact
- that I gotta live like this
Until, I don't wish stupid shit - like that I had been born rich
Instead of a broke bitch
Waiting for the landlord to knock - So, I can tell him that I
ain't got all the rent ... again
and get it over with
Just one of my everyday drama's that don't make no sense
-Shit , my check ain't even cashed and it's been spent
..But I do have four dollars ... and a few cents
So - So what if I wanna kick it with my best friend gin ?
Fall in the bottle she's wrapped in 'til we're both trapped and I'm drunk again
... and it's even better when ol' Mary Jane can drop in
... Cause she's free for the weekend - or pimpin' me for ten or twenty of my dividends
'Cause she know she makes me feel so good that
I'm a Mara- Lesbian
So what if I go into a trance
- drop my pants and do a handstand ?
Black out in church - hike up my skirt and give a lapdance ?
I'm the life of the party
- Teach you how to be naughty
- make you glad that you met me
- AND I'LL DRINK
WHEN I'M
READY

Spit [spit] – *slang verb* (used without object)

1. To say, speak, talk
2. To sing or rap
3. To eject from the mouth
4. To set a flame to (i.e. what a superb lyricist can do to a mic)

- Slang*etry definition

1. To speak from the heart about a subject of vast importance
2. What I wanna do right now :

I Wanna Spit

-I wanna spit until I don't wanna cry no more

-I wanna spit until there's NO such thing as WAR

-I wanna spit to get away from the soldiers cry's...and my own "Lord why's"...

-I wanna spit until I change history, misery, poverty,

incestry, child molesting, the music industry,

- and a government that spins the truth into make believe...

I wanna spit until I've tear drenched faces and made changes-

I wanna spit - until every word in the dictionary falls out of my breath and I can't say shit else – I WANNA SPIT THE WORLD OPEN AND INTRODUCE MYSELF

-I wanna spit until the last word stated leaves space vacated and souls medicated

- I wanna spit so hard that I feel touched by God

-I wanna spit until time re-arranges and BRINGS OUR HEROES back, spit the mothers off crack

- spit this load off my back...spit our souls back on track

- I wanna spit little pregnant girls' stomach's back flat

-..and if I can never spit like that - I'll spit enough so that they will know that a bulging belly is only

a bump in the road- another hand to hold- a chance to mine gold but,

-I wanna spit the daddy's back through the doors un-ashamed, un-shackled and un-blamed. 'Cause I'mo spit 'em back , with their souls changed and their mind's re-arranged, integrity reclaimed, understanding ingrained, they gone be soul saved and black history trained...so their smiles don't feel strange to children who never knew their names...-I wanna spit back open the church doors

♠♥♦♣

- Spit until I find that one endless sentence with just the right words...

-I wanna spit to say what I mean and mean what I say, I wanna spit me and my family into some brighter days...

-and I wanna spit about my kids 'cause their names are etched into my skin- in ink of Indian, and the love is born in- I wanna spit until *they* don't wanna cry no more- I wanna spit until *they* free- Because, the same things I spit for myself – I wanna spit for them 'til my last breath- I wanna spit 'cause they carry mama's name- and carry mama's thang's and kiss mama into sweet dreams-

-I wanna spit him into the next Martin Luther King and spit her 'til she can earn her own rings and buy her own things - I wanna spit until they understand that there is a Father on high who will never leave - so high He sees their every need, He will never leave, promised in His word that He will never deceive – and never need a reprieve and He's only as far away as their knees...-I wanna spit until there's always presents on birthdays...Spit this soul flow until I can't think of a single soul thing else to say - 'cause when I think about my last few pennies spent- my due rent- these last and evil days and this economy shit

I WANNA SPIT

THE DOWNLOW GUIDE:

They call it downlow
Because, it's low down what you do
You cover so much deceit under a smile so sweet
You know just how much charm to turn on - to turn a bitch weak
Always know the right thing to say and do
Camouflaged in yo' expensive colognes
- that attracts chicks like pheromones
so, you got a bitch hanging on each arm
- in uniform as a sexy metro sexual
who lay good pipe cause you try -sexual
Few know you undercover bisexual
A.K.A. if you like dick + have dick = you homosexual
I don't get it really -why you deceive these girls the way you do
& they're all so glittery & pretty
But -all yo' boyfriends are pretty too
Tall, strong and sexy just like you
Look like they got money and good dick just -like you do
& they know all the tricks – 'cause they slick- like you too
Got that 'come get me' earring under they lip- like you do
.......Right ear pierced for the old school
But you swear you ain't gay
Either prison, God or your demons made you this way
So, you'll take a little penis if that's what's going for the day...
Or hunt it down 'cause you need it in the worst kind of way
Then go home and kiss yo' main chick in the face
Got her living in the front of your closet with you
Where you hang your, "real boy" suits
(And R. Kelly can sing anything
Except about the darkest part of that closet,
   – cause his voice can't even go that deep)
you tell that bitch to swim –and she leap
- and she done got almost all the 'h's from you
From herpes to hepatitis
 Three kids and that bitch gone get arthritis
Tryna hold on to you
fighting chicks all around town
'Cause you dickin' them down too

If they down for the oral then you down too
Then put a condom on like something man - made can protect you
& don't none of y'all get tested or nothing
Unless there's symptoms of something
just a repetitive, deceptive process
wrap up another bitch and put her in the mix
With you and yo' downlow bros -and all they chicks
    -and all the other niggas
        they sleeping wit'
you a sex junkie-gotta have yo' fix
 - not only do you gotta have *all* the icings on ya cakes and eat 'em too
U gotta put ya dick in the chocolate pudding bowl, *and* lick the beaters *& the* spoons
You greedy motherfucker you
Now, if you got to keep yo sexuality on the D.L.
Don't ask & don't tell
We all get it, just don't be so low down with it
- just let a chick know
Before you get her tangled in yo' down low
So -that her decision to be your woman is consensual
Based in honesty that's mutual - it may be unconventional
'but it ain't about what nobody thinks –it's about what the two of *y'all* know
And you may find out some things *you* don't know
While you think you so smart
If you open up and have that good heart to heart
You'll see, your girl might be into that kind of thang
–or she's just that into you
So, that whatever turns you on turns that bitch on too
You might find out she on *her own* type of downlow
and was wondering how to tell **you ...**
A little truth can cause a massive break-through
'Cause the lie might be the crux of all the shit that y'all go through
 Now this poem ain't at all about my <u>regular gay dudes</u>
You've decided who you are- which is hard enough ...therefore hell, you just wanna do you
alot of y'all will testify that them down lows will get y'all too
Sneak you at the gay club
    -The way them downlows do
With that story 'bout how he's so glad he finally met someone like you
      - or how he just so confused...
You end up outing him to his woman
- cause them cowards can't tell the truth
- you just wanted to be down & looked around

and that mofo had done downlow'd you too
You poor baby you...
And ladies ya'll know, I wouldn't let this pen go
Without giving you a few signs of the Down Low
If it was crossing yo' mind, and you wasn't sure about your man's tendencies
Then I think it's about time that you know:

SOME SIGNS OF THE DOWNLOW
If he Tivo's soap operas for when he get's home
Frequently come up missing and he can't be reached by phone
And all the other chicks he usually run through
        are calling yo' phone looking for him too
There you go -
You probably tangled in the down low
If when you cry that nigga crying too
That ain't moral support child
The man in him generally don't know what the fuck to do
'cause when he grows up – he wanna be like you
When you gone from home- he probably lounge around in yo' lingerie and shoes
So what, he cook and clean and go shopping with you?
-girl, it ain't yo fault , he done tricked other chicks too
'that's what them sheisty, shifty motherfuckers do
According to the rules ....
You ain't just got a you an **EXTRA SENSITIVE** dude
Girl no- you got a **DOWNLOW**
Now them **UNDERCOVER THUGS**
With them mean mugs
 are a little harder to peep out
They got the same Tims and tattoos
and the same attitude
as the rest of the crew
They don't follow the same meticulous patterns as the other downlows do
He may not bathe or shave for a couple of days
And his hair might be nappy too
But, he clean up good when he do
And girl , we already know that when he take off his clothes
- that nigga is gone be sexy than a motherfucker too
And love you real hard and grimy -like them thug niggas do
One big clue for them is if they always '*just got out*'
They'll rape a nigga in the bathroom if they catch him out

♠ ♥ ♦ ♣

Get with they '*just got out too* ' niggas and brag about it

And they "Ain't checkin for no bitches, 'cause that cash is what they 'bout !"

(They yell that shit with attitude when they in the hood hanging out)

Though they get more head in dark alleys -than cash pay out

And if you watch him -the way you should

He kind of stand apart from the other dudes

 -just looking, trying to make some eye contact

Or blatantly bringing up his jail house sex

Looking round the crew see who wanna be next

When he wit you he a little rude -But, the only reason y'all together anyway is cause when you texted him- he texted back to you

Quick to call you bitch , but that's what jail niggas do

-plus, you attract that shit with yo' attitude (but, hey that's you)

-when it comes to him – don't keep it twisted ,Girl

 You probably hooking up with a downlow thug

And if you've even been with someone for awhile now

and some thing's about his personality –have always seemed a little 'off' somehow…

Like, sometimes you feel like he's in his own zone

 -like he frequently fakes his sex moans

 And sometimes he can only get turned on by doing freaky shit, like sticking things in yo' brown zone - or tryna stick things in his own …

 If his lock & key collection includes one gay porn

 If him and his homeboy sit way closer than the norm

 play fight and grab each other in the groin

 If this same homie can usually get more love from your man -than you

 Then BINGO – you probably got a downlow

-and another clue you can bet on

 If he got pictures you can't unlock on his phone

 Or a penis show up as a 'prank gone wrong'

Don't make him waste his breath and tell you no more - girl, he's on the downlow

Back to my ladies :

& if you single and a dude walks up to you

Ain't a hair out of place

and his eyebrows waxed too

His eyeballs is twinkling at you

either hazel or blue -

Don't let that shit distract you

If them shit's are contacts girl tell that downlow devil to flee from you

if the color is not synthetic look *waaaay* downlow - and see if

His t-shirt match exactly with his shoes

if that nigga is groomed better than you

and wanna groom you too

98.99 times I'm just telling you ….

Even if you wanna think you just found that one man who is actually too good to be true…

-The Downlow is coming for you

Now if you mad about this poem it's probably about you

Sitting in yo' closet with ya g-string twisted 'cause you know I'm tellin' the truth

& I'm sorry you gotta feel that way -maybe one day the truth will set you free

but for now re-direct that shit to yo' situation and don't try to put it on me

you're tragically fucked up –we all agree

hell, a bitch can't tell whether you're a trick or a treat

but that's just the you – that you are currently

you can always be better if you choose to be

and to my girls- you got 'The Guide' now -so don't be that game he tryna play

Dumbfounded & blindsided and left crying at the end of the day

Sniffling through tissues -trying to find clues in old pictures

That 'you should have known', ain't the issue

'Cause if you don't watch out girl -them Downlows Will - Get -You

CALL ME

I just wanted to tell y'all this one I wrote one night...about one of my last love's
...'Cause he was on my mind at the time
I remember that nigga used to have my heart singing all off key like...
"I can't get you out my mind
... I think about you all the time
...Why don't you call me ?
.... Don't you wanna call me ?
... Please won't you call me ?....."
Then I would just drown in the silence of my phone without his ring....
...then when my cravings really took control
I would drunk dial his number and hang up the phone
...He would see my nickname scrawled across his caller id
then he would press send...and he would call me
And he'd be like, 'Hey girl, where you been ?"
-like *he* had been looking for *me* -and just the sound of his voice would make my knees go weak
So, even though my mind would disagree...my skin would scream:
Laying here meltin' in sin... waiting for you to come jump in ....And he would say he was coming over...and that when he got by my house, he was gone...call me
Then he would come over with that look - he knew would melt me all over
- He would say all the words he knew would help him get over
he would...touch every spot, that he knew by heart...that I loved all over
-then take his little pieces of me and disappear all over
I'm talking 'bout -that nigga had me laying down the history for Usher songs
- 'Cause...a bitch had it bad
I was stuck in the house - I didn't wanna have fun
– because, that nigga was <u>all</u> I was thinking about
Until, one day I realized I was tired of his shit
Him calling me at one in da morning - like I was just his hit
all I could get -was his rare texts and his spare sex
He would hit me up when he needed my kind of love – then he was on to the next
I knew that boy wouldn't ever love me – but it was only when it came to him,
that I saw where I wasn't loving myself
- plus, my daddy always told me that I was a queen
 so, it was furthermore behavior unbecoming - to be treated thusly
So, I cleaned away his memory in drastic steps

I threw away all the t-shirts that he left that I had kept, 'cause they smelt like the times he had touched me...

I burned all of the pictures that used to mean so much - watched the smoke scorch those happy smiles that used to be my love crutch, something tangible that I could touch- when I hadn't seen his ass in weeks. I let the ash blow away with a smile on my face and stomped what was left under my feet

- And then I left his ass a note on the door - in big block letters that he couldn't ignore

It said : IF YOU LOOKING FOR A GOOD TIME THEN BYPASS ME - CAUSE THERE'S A BRAND NEW WOMAN SLEEPING IN THIS BED AND AIN'T NO VACANCIES . NOW I APPRECIATE ALL THE LITTLE THANGS THAT YOU BOUGHT ME AND ALL THE LESSONS THAT YOU TAUGHT ME , LIKE THE FACT THAT I CAN'T LIVE WITH YOU KILLING ME SOFTLY , SO NIGGA -BACK UP OFF MY PORCH AND UP OFF ME.

So, the next time he saw me - his eyes picked me out the throng

I had my baddest jeans on and my hips was singing this song:

'Hey don't you like that ?
Tell me don't you miss that ?
Wish you could come back
But baby don't call me.'

Drunk Textin (Again)

I deleted yo' number for self-preservation...
To negate my proclivities for drunken textation

With poetry about missing yo' lips

and yo' fingertips

& tellin you how much I wanna 'f' you...

found myself drunk textin' you at the club

and on da bus

Sippin' vodka all day getting fucked up

Trying not to think about us

Not about our history 'cause there wasn't that much

Because, we was over before we even got started

Which is why I be textin' you like I'm retarded

'Cause a bitch tipsy & can't barely see

36858863 for "do you (still) love me?"

When I know you never did

I just remember us kissing in the dark

- two zippers apart

And get pipe dreams about having yo' kids

and start drunk textin' again

Thinking up schemes to get next to you

& dat Vodka be hollin "Gul, you know what to do

Text him and see if he thinkin' about you too.."

That's why I erased yo number

So, I'd quit waiting for yo' ringtone to wake me up out my slumber

Talking 'bout some ," *Boy I need you bad as my heartbeat, bad like the food I eat, bad as the air I breathe...*"

Some bitch I don't even know brainwashing me

To the point where - you couldn't even wake me up 'cause thinking about you- I can't sleep

& we was only together a few weeks

But, it was strange

I swear that everywhere I looked I saw your name

Like the elements was telling me you was supposed to be my man

And the funny thang, is that *I let u* go 'cause I saw yo' game

At first, I put on my poker face

And tried to bluff you into thinking I was a whole 'nother bitch

The type you needed to be with

- hoping your opinion- of what I could be to you would switch

After u dropped that big secret bout yo' main chick

Clued me in that you was being slick &

Tryin' to play in my brain

So, she could get all the good shit -and I'd be yo' on the side thang

Da chick that has no name

While she get the ring and the sweet nothings

With me stuck tryna make our nothing into something

... more than just chilling and humping

And since I find myself needing to be touched by you again

Chugging down Vodka, I'm a mess again

I'm tryna see if I can find yo' number somewhere...so I can text you again

Candy Had A Problem

Candy had a lot of problems - she would do anything , ride any ding a ling
Looking for something or someone that could solve 'em
Cause' candy's main problem was her damn self
The ghosts that chased her every day were reflections of herself
Her head was a brick wall-with 'I ain't listening' graffiti'd on
& she took every step on her road of life anticipating a fall
Because that girl was scared of her greatness
Scared of being alone
Scared nobody would love her with the lights on
She was scared of everything
And scared of nothing
Cause 'Candy, deep down, was fearless...
She was angry with all men
Yet, she craved their nearness
'Cause they were validation to her,
That she was somebody
She didn't even know 10 times 10
She dropped out of school so her real education could begin
But she could estimate every baller by the size of his rims
She could calculate how to get herself next to him- then get intimidated all over again
Cause' candy had a problem
Her problem was her mama - who didn't teach her shit
So, she used her coochie like a change machine trying to get rich
So she could stunt in front of her home girls with her new- nigga bought shit
Everybody knew she was open for all holes, couldn't hear the name Candy without hearing,
"Mayne, you gotta show her the money first-
      after that -anything goes"

Cause' Candy's main life goal - was being bigger & better than her heroes -which was video hoes ... and chicks that swung around on stripper poles
Making that flossy, drift through they fingers type dough
That would eventually drift up their nose -in white dopes...
Candy saw it every day and still refused to know
'That she was the same little girl, that they were...blowing through life out of control..
just looking for daddy... or like Candy - a product of his unusual sex..
She was loud and wild so she stayed surrounded by niggas that didn't show her no respect
'Cause the only word they knew how to call her - was bitch
Anybody who ever told her they loved her - was tricks
So...a person...could understand her problems
I stood around with her one day trying to help her solve them
But her mind was too re-arranged for me
This is what Candy told me – "I stand around in broad daylight and darkness is all I see
You tell me there's a God on high
- but, ain't got no proof for me
Ain't no God that I can see - & no way you can make me believe
That some, Being - up in a word as sweet as heaven, would pave these dirty streets
and make this type of life - for me to have to lead
-' she looked so sad when she said to me...' Un uh ,' ain't no God in this place "...
And I was thinking only a God who had mastery of angels - could have created her face .
So, I asked her , "Well, Candy - what other way could you have come to **Be** - from a microscopic piece of jelly?"
She said, "A donation from a man who wasn't shit -
A contribution to my mama's belly, for her swirling around on his dick - so she could get another crack hit, 'what ?'- Though the tears in her eyes belied, her shoulder shrug, I could see that Candy needed to see a lot of things, the main thing I could show her was some love...My arms pulled her into a soft hug on their own accord but, she couldn't connect with the feeling, so she pushed me away with a look that killed me
then went with her speech:
"Ain't nobody ever gave a damn about me, so why u standing here tryna act like u give a fuck ?".
I looked at her and wished I had a whole' 'nother lifetime to try and tell her all the things I learned growing up
& that when she was down in the dirt, all she had to do was look up - & to place her value further than what was under her mini-skirt but , I never got the chance
by the time I got my words together - together she had got killed for messing with somebody else's man but, I heard she had a cross clutched in her hand ....
So I can only hope that Candy made it on high and He had reached her before me - Finally gave Candy some peace ...and absolved her of all her problems ...

i Never

I never finished anything but high school
And two stomach terms
I made it to 34 years but, only finished 23
My immaturity is a negative
So, I have to take a few years back
I never finished loving nobody
Or being kissed right
Or learning how to love
...properly
Or telling mama
How much I appreciate her
Or telling the world my stories
- so, still I write...
I never finished changing anything
That matters yet
- so every day I try to change myself...
I never finished my whole bottle
- So, I take a little sip every day
I never finished raising my flowers
and sometimes...
They wither at my touch
So, I water them with secret tears
And ask God to bring sunshine
I never finished laughing
So, I dig for joy
In the dark places my mind goes
I never finished the perfect poem
But, I will – when I finish achieving
I never finished praying
& I won't as long as I'm breathing
I never finished – crying
Because, tears will always be
To purge until we're free
I never finished trying
I refuse until, I cease...

♠ ♥ ♦ ♣

I LOVE YOU

I love you so much that I wrote…I love you + plus your name + mine…a trillion times…until, the words blurred together and spelled = FOREVER…

Then, I buried the pages under a rosebush in a soft rain and kissed all the petals until night came and under every kiss, I whispered

–I love you…because it's true…

I love you in a way that could only be described by Eve, when Adam gave his rib so that she could breathe. But, you gave me your entire heart without a thought. That's why I love you….

I even lay around naked outside sometimes - so, that nothing man made come between my thoughts of you and the night sky…and my praises for you to the Most High - I probably look like a fool - but no one even bothers to ask me why…because…they know it has something to do…with my love for you…As the breeze accepts my skin under the shooting stars, I wish I love you's to you again and again, as I watch them fall. Because, I love you so much - that it seeps from my skin like passion fruit in one of Heavens gardens. So, that the un-loved breathe our essence…and believe in God…I love you so much that it hurts my heart just to feel your touch. But, that's okay. Some people would give anything to feel this sweet a pain, just one time…to be loved in kind…the way

I *L*OVE YOU

DEADBEAT POETRY

I'm writing deadbeat poetry on these child support papers…

My calm hand, doesn't waiver

'Cause I'm writing my soul flow across your name

Hoping to never see it again

And page after page

I'm writing the sourness of this document into lemonade

And making the bitterness sweet…

I've acquired a taste for the drink

If it were up to you

It'd be a nasty brew – ain't that true?

'Cause being nasty and belligerent is what you do–

I'm writing over the words of what you're putting me through

In dark black ink, unaffected by you

But, nourished by the inspiration

Of such an ugly situation

As you and the things you do

And the turmoil you put our child through

With your careless attitude

You'd rather stay wrong, than even try at doing good

As customary

You're unrepentant and contrary

You got thousand dollar speakers, that pump hits of idiots

Screaming 'Baby mama's ain't shit"

But, what is a deadbeat that inspires poetry?

Collaborates in ho-etry?

Lives to deceive

and doesn't care

where his child...breathes

- what he plans to achieve

- don't have an idea where he lays his head

if he's being fed

he could be dead

While you're lost off in your own world

spreading your seeds to the next girl

When I think about- who ain't shit

You're who the description fits- to me

You should feed your mind on this baby-mama-ology

The logic that gives me this peace

While you go out of yo' way to initiate emotional brawls

And try to leave me with scars

So, go ahead and hit me one more time

The pleasure is all mine

'Cause I'm still gone stand strong

- hold on tight to my baby and move on

'Cause I know about your own scars

That run way deeper than ours...

some of your mental scars I put there myself

the kind band-aids , Bactene , therapy

and Mama's kisses won't help

And also, it's evident

From the time you've spent

Acting stupid with me for my child to see

That what came from my womb

Will never love you...

'Cause, anytime his thoughts on you have to be explained

now, he uses your first name...

Though, he probably does yearn for you

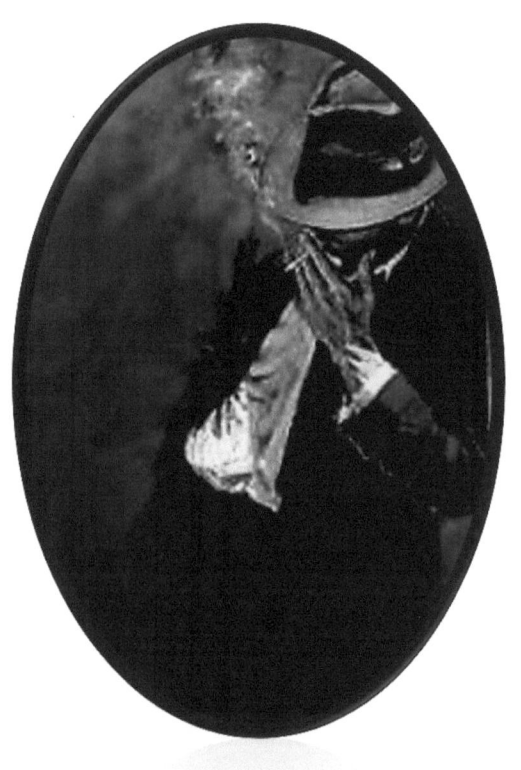

Just hates the things you do

- And you could be the type

To change one day and do right

wake up one day

And regret that you made it this way

But, probably not

That would take too much sense, that I know you ain't got

So, while I'm speaking on you, just this one time

With this one rhyme

I just have to say

Before, I ended the page

Thanks for never showing up at my house

With your bad vibe and your dark clouds

And again for this child

Who does me proud…

Of course, your thanks goes on this court decree

- which means nothing to me

But… *Deadbeat Poetry*

A Single Mama's Prayer

When everything's falling apart, Lord
Let me keep it together
& remember to praise you every time I see the sky
- no matter what the weather
Send your Holy Ghost & your angel's down
to guide us through this day
& give us peace when we pray
Let us sleep…sweet when we lay
& Lord, Please - help me to raise these kids
Bless their natural father wherever he is
and whatever he has chosen to do…
If he refuses to know his children
Please Lord, Let Him Know You
& please control my flesh - You know that's my struggle every day
And help me discipline my mind - until I'm more like You in every way
Let my words drip like honey
& my name - like fine ointment
Let my destiny be - more than I can dream
Because, You appointed it
In the same tone -
as when You said "Let There Be Light"- and the sun shone
And, Lord, please forgive me for all of the wrongs that I've done
Let this prayer come to you pure as I kneel at your throne
Please keep me and give my family…a portion of your blessings
I am so longing for your favor
…let some drops fall on me
Let me be the best mother that I can be
Let me not bow down to sin -
Because these kids look up to me
Give me wisdom when I speak
And let me practice what I preach
…Make my kisses extra sweet
Lord, bless the work of these hands &
Let me walk with love, grace, joy and intelligence
If you could, Father - Send on that good man
-Amen

Mama

When my legs were just a thought in another man's reality

Mama, you carried me

When I saw my first hint of the sun

You were the ray of light

When I didn't know arms

I knew your embrace

On your breast I found my security

my serenity, my identity

In your smile, God answered the question that I knew not how to ask

They rejoiced the squeal of a newborn child

Only you knew the meaning

You heard me call your name...

Mama...

Invisible Butterfly

Invisible Butterfly
Always in someone else's sky
U fly through so many springs
On those delicate wings
That catch air and flutter
With their translucent colors
Those other exotic things
That float haughtily when the wind breathes
Don't have the wings that you grew....
...Or love the flowers like you do
Such a pretty little butterfly
Can't wait 'til I reach my eyes
And see your rise
on wings that grew so strong that they split the sky...
and aerodynamic so they death defy
so beautiful that they mesmerize
Because, though it seems that no one else can see
You are, it's clear to me
The loveliest butterfly in season
If for no other reason
While you flew through the noon's
Than that you broke from your cocoon

I Won't Eat 'Til U Love Me Again

I won't eat 'til U love me…again

-I'm going to lay in the middle-

of this empty hole in my soul

…And caress your picture…

I'll let my lips fade away

If I can't kiss you…

I will refuse to speak

If I can't say, I love you

and your name…

in the same phrase

to your face…

Because, I need you

Like the air

needs the wind…to breath

like a greedy man-

…need's everything

So, not even a morsel will cross my teeth

Until, I waste away…

I swear in a blood oath - signed this day

That I won't eat until U love me…again

I NEED YOU TO HOLD ME LOOSELY

I need you to hold me loosely
Your arms are starting to feel like a noose to me
'Cause you holding on too...tightly
& your calls are becoming a nuisance
honestly
Not that heart crashing shit that it used to be
because it happens so constantly
until
I feel like you playing tug of war with telephone lines
Try'na pull me over to yo' side
drag me into your frame of mind
When hardheaded me getting sucked in
- to whatever dream world you stuck in
Is on a long list of future things - that won't ever happen
& you're making all that a distraction
When all I need
is for you to
... Hold me loosely ...
I just need to be told I'm beautiful sometimes ...
And have things stroked & be touched
once and awhile, Chile
But, even my body language don't say forever
So, stop planning out how we gone be together
And how you gone move me to some state
that I ain't ever wanted to be
- away from my family
So, we can buy a big house and live tax free
Boy, you crazy
You so set on yo plans to give me all the things
That I never wanted or asked for - and don't need
That you can't see
that my focus ain't money and material things...
pretty much , all the things I love in life are free
And if you'd ever been listening to me
You'd know that the type of man I need to love me

Ain't got to have much really ....
A nice body
And a personality that's suited to me
and sometimes he'll let me be the big spoon
So, I'll know that even when we sleep
he can still be depended on to
be held on to...
the kind of man that'll pray with me...
While you don't take God seriously
I need the kind of man that - when we up
We gone be up together
When we broke - we gone laugh & love until things get better
We gone sit in the dirt together and look up
hold hands & not give up
on anything...
Get lost somewhere in each other's eyes
and refuseto come back right away
His kiss will take my breath away ...
And you don't make me feel none of those ways ...
So , Nigga ... hold me loosely
& Quit talking 'bout you wanna marry me
How yo' mama keep saying we was 'meant to be'
'Cause   she claim - she saw our wedding in a dream
Boy, you can't find a big enough ring
To bind me in a house with you
- and all the things I don't like - that you do
Seems like don't nothing be getting through
when I be telling you , that you ain't the one for me
Instead of us suffocating in your emotions
-why can't you let me breathe & let us be..
and just ...I need you to
.... hold me loosely....
I just wanna have some laughs in yo' bed
Watch t.v. while I stroke yo' head
Talk to you when I need to de-stress
Be amazed every time you undress
But, we ain't gone make it -
unless...
You hold me loosely...

DEAR SIR

(A POEM ABOUT WHY BABY'S DADDYS PROBABLY CAN'T STAND ME)
Based on absolutely Real Facebook messages...
I swear I couldn't make this shit up

* The more I try to finish this book, I swear the more it keeps writing itself. I know I shouldn't do this shit, but I wrote it 'cause can't nobody else ...sound like that angry black woman that we baby's mamas become sometimes. When a motherfucker - you may or may not have used to have loved - talks to you like he done lost what was left of his mind. Don't appreciate how hard you be trying or he's the kind that don't do shit for you but - give you a free piece of his mind. The baby's mamas who gone read this true conversation and think they been through this same type of conversation a few times. Or probably been through baby daddy situations way worse than mine .... This is ain't so much a poem - as it is part of my all true baby mama story- based on Facebook lines ...

THE BABY'S DADDY (whose name is left out to protect the innocent – not him of course, the innocent)
March 28 at 6:01am
T .T. I told I told you I needed to talk to you, and I want to talk to my daughter , please give me a call, or let here call me.
Sent via Facebook Mobile

T.T King April 3 at 1:21am
Dear Sir,
 I'm updating the pics on my Facebook page, so you can see an updated version of your childs face, since you seem so agitated
 though you don't know and can't spell her middle name
and ain't never called (or even sent a card) on a birthday.
And I passed along the message that you sent and the phone number,
hopefully you old enough to not wonder
why she don't care to call.
And if you don't , let me just tell you that it's because it's so evident that you don't care at all
But, I can't keep having the same conversations about it that's why I didn't write back at all..
I just told her yesterday that she has your laugh and that dimple and she's hoping she'll be tall like you.
You're welcome to Facebook her a message any time and I promise I'll put it right through. I been out of this thing for a long time boy- THE REST OF YOU AND HER IS UP TO YOU.<-I put that shit in bold letters to make sure the words get through :)

I wrote you this poem off the top of my head cause it's all I could do ...
and you probably didn't even know it was a poem, 'cause nigga you ain't never got a clue
 (lmfao @you)
Now that you get it -
You'll probably write me one back that says : fuck you lol but, that's cool.. that's you.
Hopefully, you've grown up and will just start to hit her up and let her get to know you , the way your other kids do.
I swear on everything this is the last thing I'll probably ever say to you.
But like I said, any message you would like to send – I swear I'll send it right through.

T.T. KING April 3 at 10:09am Report
THE BABY'S DADDY : Yes and I guess your lil smart ass made all the right decisions in life, but she's growing up and you right it want have anything to do with you, it seems like your going to be a bitter person all your little life.
Sent via Facebook Mobile

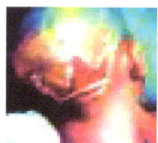

T.T. King April 4 at 1:09pm
Dang boy, that was a whole paragraph you could have written to her and for her. You're welcome to do so at any time-I PROMISE I'LL GET IT RIGHT TO HER. No matter what it says.

(* and etcetera... I showed a lot of restraint not getting into the fact that I'm not bitter I'm blessed, 'cause I ain't got time for that boy and his mess... notice there was a curse word thrown in there, on his part-but, <u>not one</u> thank you. That's alright though, I'm still praying that God touch him.)

- *-Update : Y'all I swear I wasn't going to print any more of our conversation. Then- I opened this:*

THE BABY'S DADDY: Well you didn't accept me as a friend yet, do I could see them.
Sent via Facebook Mobile

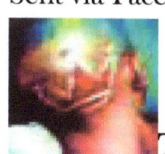**T.T. King** April 7 at 3:28pm
 You're Welcome. (my response after re-adding him)

THE BABY'S DADDY April 7 at 3:39pm Report
Are you gone let here call me, or you gone give me your number miss king**.**

(Now to those of us, who can spell the word her (and won't ...and 'you're: plural for you are) did y'all not clearly read me tell that boy in bold letters to write her ? -That I did give her his number

and the message? Why the fuck would she want him to call her when he won't take time to get to know her & let her get to know him? More, than that, how does **he** not get that? And most importantly –How is this boy thirty something years old and can't spell?

Anyway... y'all see, he called me 'miss king' at the end. He was trying to be cute but, he got the idea from me so at least he learned something today.– So, in an effort to stay lady-like in this situation- I didn't respond to his last message and don't plan on doing so. Since, this book is like therapy , this is the message **I wish** I could have sent him back but, I didn't –keep in mind I didn't :

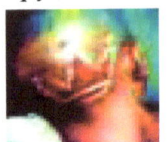

T.T. King *(The immature message that I wish the new me -would let the old me-in me send :)*
Dear Sir,

I told you I updated the fucking pictures –and tried to be nice about it

Even though, I already knew you was gone act stupid choose one word and try to start a fight about it

I even looked past your mis-typed attitude -and the general shitty motherfucker you've been and re-added yo' simple ass, as my Facebook friend

Even though friends not even a category I can ever see us in, again

    & I did all these things expediently and benevolently

So, I don't know what the fuck else you want from me

& NO- you <u>cannot</u> have my number- 'cause I'm the one who pays the bill

And don't ever want the displeasure of hearing your voice on the other end...

I'm just gone sit back and wait out this 'tryna communicate', blue moon you're in..

watch another one of your weak attempts to rebuild and re-burn the same bridge

..then walk over the ashes with yo' other kids

I Am Convinced That You Are An Idiot. Period

So, I had her make her own page so she could discuss things herself with you

'Cause I ain't got the time or inclination to be tryna keep dealing with you

I hope you accepted her friend request, cause with me yo' ass is re-unfriended and re-discontinued

and I'm re-blocking your messages as soon as I get back online

The woman in me, that believe in the Lord, was just trying to give you some time to see her request and respond...

I hope if I ever have to speak to you again... He done re-calibrated yo' mind ..... as well as mine

So, I could ever share more than ten words with you -without wanting to slap the shit out of you numerous times....

* *I can't close out this book without thanking him though because, he's one of the reasons I am what I am. So, thank you Stupid and thank God for you (we won't even discuss the fact that you misspelled the word her - Facebook ain't got spellcheck and Jesus loves you).*

Walking In Mama's Shoes

I always knew that one day I would walk in mama's shoes
Do the same in front of the stove two step to mama's same
'Lord bring us some more food 'blues
- whatever I didn't know in life, those shoes would walk me to the clues
I would put them on and my womans' mind would know exactly what to do...
Because, I always knew that one day mama's shoes would fit my feet
That's why I watched her before I could speak
Learned how to do the 'back of the bra strap reach'
how to say, "Amen!" when the preacher preach
how to be strong but, yet meek
how to kiss a man on da cheek and make his knees go weak...
'Cause when I contemplated mama's shoes I could feel
that the magic was in the heels...
I knew whenever I put those shoes on
I would understand the words to love songs
and sing along while I put my lipstick on
'bout how that no good man done did me wrong
While I dabbed my neck with sweet cologne
And smoothed on lotion until my skin shone
Beause, that's what I saw mama do
In her black slip and those shoes
So - I just knew
that those heels would be my body's exclamation points
accentuate the swivel of my hip joints
and walk me through a few strange beds
Just like even my mama's- mama's - mamas...shoes did
And my woman shoes would strut me past the no good men
- to the one that was absolutely real
Watching mama walk I learned to stride with purpose and the truth
That's why my footfalls sound off like attitude...
And if the pace is real hard – it usually means I'm coming for you
And when shit gets thick
I can give the back of these heels two clicks - make a wish
... and be back home again
All I gotta do... is call mama on the phone again
Let her voice remind the child in me, that ... I ain't alone again

Let her nourish me with her wisdom
then ... I'm on my own again
I shed some inner light on what I didn't do right
so, I don't get it wrong again
Press repeat on my stereo...and play my song again
- then I figure out which way to point these heels and baby - it's on again
So, even though mama's shoes are still too big for my feet to fill
Like I said - now I got my own pair of woman heels
So, just like her I sling my babies around my hip
Making corn bread and breast milk
& I make my own rules- pay my own dues
& stroll away from conversation of all fools ....
while I'm walking in mama's shoes

Dedication's

I AM COMPLICATED, SELFISH SOMETIMES; CRAZY AND HAVE NO SELF CONTROL - Thank God there's still people that can love me anyway - THIS BOOK IS DEDICATED TO Y'ALL. YOU KNOW I LOVE YOU BACK.

First and foremost, my baby's no matter how much bigger you get than me:

Trey and Kisura

THIS BOOK IS DEDICATED : To Trey -Boy, you laugh just like yo daddy , and act just like me -And I still wonder where you get it from … A perfect mixture of yo' whole family tree but, of course , of 'Treys' there can only be one- my son .You hate my stuff so probably will never read even this first dedication poem..Though this part specifically for you and everything we've been through…While I'm standing here amazed at your break-through and ,the fact that I helped in creating you. You're six feet tall to my 4"11 and in a few ways I look up to you. I don't do some of the things that I used to do – because of some knowledge you kicked even in your youth… it's another poem in this book that will verify what I stand by –that one of the best parts of me is you. So, I'm proud of the man you're becoming though, I'll always see your baby face…Trey. And Kisura- whose name means beautiful- you know this is all dedicated to you too. The one so quiet, yet deep enough to swim through. Don't trip about the man who left you , mature enough to know it's not just about the journey we go through -but the people who take the time to walk with you… and you the light we follow through your quiet sometimes. Hold your own part of a home down – the one that don't just notice the frown.. but cares about it. Baby, you go through life so sweet and ain't complete unless you somewhere around me. They say can't nobody else get close to you 'cause I keep you so close under my wing , but everybody smart -knows to stay close to beautiful things, I just happened to have one that was born to me…And to mama- I don't mean to be redundant but, it all comes back to you -' cause I'm you in abundance. The root to my tree the one who keeps me grounded spiritually and hold me down in the seasons when all my leaves leave, them ones that blew away in the breeze. Besides, God you are the thing I'll always believe. Always wear dresses cause you old testament and know you have to separate yourself in order to lead…You taught me greatness in independence and that prayer will get me through this thing and not to just have the faith of a mustard seed but, of the biggest oak in Yosemite. **And to my daddy** - jack of all trades and lingual master of everything -the best absent father that God had for me...always a phone call away so it's like you stayed with me- and made sure you didn't get off the phone until I was sure I knew everything...IN THE WORLD . A card every September for 35 years, though I've only seen your face a few times but, your voice has wiped away my tears and toughened me up from my fears so many times....You are that constant voice that the girl in me will always need ..and the woman in me will always heed.. and thank you because the wisest parts of me- came from you. I get this artistic thing from you too, so you know what it means to me. When I look back through our history, it came to me that I was meant to be.. you're what every father who can't be there physically should strive to be....(TO MY READERS CHECK OUT MY DAD'S ART ONLINE Sometime- JAHN BRONSON- HE'S AMAZING).And of course, this dedication is to **Angie** when everybody else run - you stand with me. My best friend who always understand -when don't nobody else get me .'Told me "Girl, just come home.", when I was defeated-and my own family didn't give a damn about nothing I needed-didn't care that I was beat down ,broke down and f'd up-couldn't bother to be tainted with my bad luck. -You Angie –you- that old Cancer girl with that true, stick like glue - kind of love- dug them claws in me and ain't never gave up ....on me or my dreams...The only person who ever read <u>everything</u> I ever wrote....Know enough to know that right now you're choked up 'cause you know my ode to you is some of the realest s*** I ever wrote.. We got that stuff can't nobody else join in cause when we met somehow we was born in ... the reason I'm immortalizing our friendship in pen .I re-did these dedications because my first draft didn't say enough about you ... and all the people that I love-: Jossy, Jayden ,Xavier & Asia aunt T.T. put you in a verse so you can say your name was in a book that got the world shook ..and you saw me writing it in the living room –so you always know that your circumstances can never contain you... and all of you are so beautiful...To Marie & Nanna Pie (see..y'all readers don't know chasing me left me wandering aimlessly a few times) & to Lawrence the sweetest, most hustling'ist nigga I know, whenever I needed to be somewhere you was ready to go , pawned yo' stuff so I could have money for the bus and for some reason just chose to love us...which is why we will always love you...To Candace my Libra twin, who I met when you was crying and been my friend ever since... to my big headed 'nephew' Chris Washington (you know I love you boy). To Aunt Betty who let me read her books and to ALL of my Grandma's- 'cause what would a T.T. King be- if it wasn't for y'all? To J. Stokes for teaching me the meaning of: "The same thing that will make you laugh will make you cry...", but thank God if we're lucky those are some of the best laughs of your life. And to my brother Chris King- I know you had to leave so that you could get your wings - recognize my soul and know me by my new name when I see you again. Thank you for everything .... You are one of the most important things in my history and what I am presently.....(I can't put that in the past tense because I can feel your spirit around me). And a 'what's up wit 'cha – to my sisters Shelette, Detra, Dana and Licia . To the HAMPTON streets that made me and every rock, piece of pavement, and person that still has my memories stamped on it. MUCH LOVE AND RESPECT TO 'MS.KATIE' DANIELS (kiss Chris for me) , Emma Jean , Miss Lilly, Mable, Miss Siss, Peanut & Ms. Pearl 'cause these women are some of the things I will always remember about the best childhood a little country girl could ever have.

And first in my heart -**THIS BOOK IS DEDICATED TO GOD** . My lips were formed just to praise you, my life just to love you and my testimony to exalt you. ...and to any human persons I may have I forgot, charge that to my head but, definitely not to my heart. And to my fans- this book is dedicated to you... I love you too, even though we just met.....

(To my poetic heroes: Dana Gilmore, Georgia Me and Inyanla Vanzant (the poem "Today I Smiled", is a tribute to her "Yesterday I Cried" poem) and Langston Hughes, who was eloquent yet simple. To Usher and Jazmin Sullivan for the lyrics .And to all the talented graphic artists I found online for their interpretation of beauty and expression.)

I hope y'all enjoyed me as much as I loved sharing myself with you. Please keep reading with me. Slangetry II is on the way, along with my book of short stories , and a full-length fiction novel that I can't wait for y'all to read. If any of these poems touch you feel free to drop me a line on www.slangetry .com. all poets are welcome to drop some lyrics or some knowledge in the 'Slangetry Spot' on my page.

T. T. The lyrics expressed are so visionary> They will allow the reader to feel attached to the many moments that entwine a person's life whether they are an experienced person, monogamous, spiritual or someone being clued in to what is really going on! I really applaud you and would like a purchased autographed copy whenever it is released. A special person has the ability to spread the "education of life" because it is the truest sense of a classroom. Keep writing, upon the discovery of your material the masses will flood and I truly feel that everyone will be fulfilled by the artist T.T. King

- Monty Lewis

T.T. King brings new meaning to poetic lyricist. She uses her pen to write the language many women feel, but don't know how to voice. This book will make you laugh, cry, reflect, and thank God for anything that you've ever been through!

-Machell Dailey
ΔΣΘ

Excuses are Monuments of Nothingness....
Thanks for reading..
Your future favorite Poet / Author
T.T. King

© all rights reserved 2011 T.T. KING

A short Slang* glossary:

TERMS
*Ain't – am not /are not
*Cha' – you
*I'mo – I am going to
Wanna – want to
Y'all – you all ; a collective group
*Yo' – your

DEFINITIONS:

* **Baby-mama-ology**- knowledge that smart women always try to impart even and especially to their slowest 'baby's daddies'

* **Blue boyz** – police officers

* **Deadbeat** – parent that doesn't support their children, either monetarily or emotionally (i.e. dodging child support letters, getting paid under the table or illegitimate money in order to not have to officially financially support children

* **Downlow** – 1. The act of perpetrating the outward persona of heterosexuality while secretly having sexual relations with persons of the same sex 2. the act of committing a negative or underhanded act

* **Dred** – singular slang term for dreadlocks- a hairstyle where natural hair is twisted into long matted or ropelike locks.

* **Game** – 1. A series of patterned 'rules' perpetuated by a person in order to 'win' by following said rules to gain a desired result 2. convincing someone to bend to ones will and act outside of their natural character or state of being by manipulating the brain and/or emotions.

* **Hit**- A person whose sole purpose is to have physical relations with, with little other contact other than sex /or in between physical liaisons

* **Ho-etry**- The act of committing a constant series of whore-like actions (i.e. sleeping with a lot of different sexual partners, usually within a very short period of time)

* **Feds** – Federal Police Agents

* **Lame** – Person whose personality, finances or standards are not up to an acceptable social level

* **Nigga Bought Shit** – Material things purchased for a female by a male –usually as a result of 'game' or in exchange for sexual favors

* **Shiesty**- Of dubious or suspicious character (i.e. the person most likely to do some fucked up shit to you)

* **Spit**- To speak from the heart about a subject of vast importance

* **Spooning**- Sleeping position in which participants sleep with one holding the other in the chest to back position, usually with all points touching from shoulders to feet.

* **Swagger**- Confidence; Self-possessed walk reinforced by material possessions (i.e. nice clothes, car etc.)

* **The Big Spoon**- The person holding the sleeper in the spooning position.

* **Tims**- Short for timberland boots, commonly worn for fashion by urban males

* **Tracks**- Culmination line of hair in which false extensions are attached to keep hair together for weaving

* **Weave**- False hair extensions, either real (grown from human) or synthetic (made from materials) attached to the scalp for lengthening, thickening fine hair, the completion of fashion hairstyles etc.

* **Whips**- Cars; Automobiles

www.ingramcontent.com/pod-product-compliance
Lightning Source LLC
Chambersburg PA
CBHW040026050426
42453CB00002B/17